**Vocabulary ✻Tales✻**

shopping words

# Bear Goes Shopping

by Maria Fleming
illustrated by Mike Gordon

## SCHOLASTIC INC.

New York • Toronto • London • Auckland • Sydney
Mexico City • New Delhi • Hong Kong • Buenos Aires

Designed by Maria Lilja
ISBN-13: 978-0-545-08698-1 • ISBN-10: 0-545-08698-1
Copyright © 2008 by Scholastic Inc.
All rights reserved. Printed in China.

First printing, October 2008

12 11 10 9 8 7 6 5 4 3 2 1     8 9 10 11 12 13/0

Brrrr! The days are getting cold. Bear is getting sleepy. It is time to get ready for his long winter nap.

KEY WORD: **purchase**

**Simple Definition:** to buy something

**Sample Sentence:** I will *purchase* a puzzle at the toy store.

Bear can **purchase** everything he needs at the One-Stop Sleep Shop. What will Bear buy?

He rolls his cart around the store. There are a **variety** of pillows. But the white one is perfect!

**KEY WORD: choose**

**Simple Definition:** to pick something from a group of things

**Sample Sentence:** Joe is allowed to *choose* three books to take home from the library.

Look at all of the pajamas! Which pair will Bear **choose**? He picks the pajamas with snowflakes.

Bear likes these fuzzy red slippers. Uh-oh, they cost a lot! He will have to find a less **expensive** pair.

Can Bear **afford** a bedtime book? Yes!
He has enough money.

At last, Bear is done shopping. He stands in line to pay for everything.

**KEY WORD: customers**

**Simple Definition:** people who buy things

**Sample Sentence:** There are many *customers* shopping for food at the market today.

Other **customers** give Bear funny looks.
Bear just smiles at these shoppers.

Back home, Bear gets ready for bed. His new pajamas are soft and warm. His new blanket is cozy, too.

Bear is very tired, but he can't fall asleep.
Something is missing, but what?

Suddenly, Bear jumps out of bed. He grabs his **wallet** and races back to the store. He forgot to buy the most important thing. . . .

KEY WORD: **snuggle**

**Simple Definition:** to hold something close in a loving way

**Sample Sentence:** I like to *snuggle* my dog at night.

A teddy bear to **snuggle**! Soon, Bear is fast asleep, dreaming sweet dreams of spring.

# Meaning Match

**Listen to the definition. Then go to the WORD CHEST and find a vocabulary word that matches it.**

1. a group of different things
2. to pick out something from a group
3. costing a lot of money
4. to hold something close in a loving way
5. people who buy things
6. to buy something
7. to have enough money to buy something
8. a small case for holding money

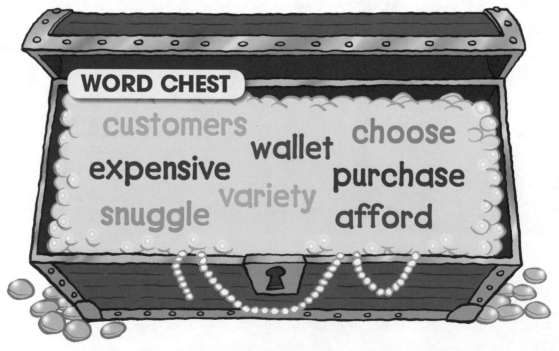

**WORD CHEST**

customers   choose

wallet

expensive   purchase

variety

snuggle   afford

Answers: 1. variety 2. choose 3. expensive 4. snuggle 5. customers 6. purchase 7. afford 8. wallet

# Vocabulary Fill-ins

**Listen to the sentence. Then go to the WORD BOX and find the best word to fill in the blank.**

**WORD BOX**

| purchase | variety | choose | expensive |
|----------|---------|--------|-----------|
| afford | customers | wallet | snuggle |

1 Can you _____ to pay $15 for that T-shirt?

2 Craig opened up his leather _____ and pulled out a dollar bill.

3 There are a _____ of different fish in the fish tank.

4 Wow! That diamond ring is very _____!

5 It's my brother's turn to _____ which movie we watch tonight.

6 When I'm sad, I _____ my stuffed rabbit to feel better.

7 They had a lot of _____ at their school bake sale.

8 My feet are growing so fast I need to _____ new shoes every year.

**Answers:** 1. afford 2. wallet 3. variety 4. expensive 5. choose 6. snuggle 7. customers 8. purchase

15

# Vocabulary Questions

**Listen to the question. Think about it. Then answer.**

1. What things could you **purchase** at a hardware store? How about at a bakery?

2. If you saw a penguin, a monkey, and a seal at a pet store, which would you **choose** to buy? Tell why.

3. Name three things that are **expensive**. Name three things that are NOT **expensive**.

4. How could you make money to buy a toy that you could not **afford**?

5. Do you have a stuffed animal you like to **snuggle**? Tell about it.

6. Is it good to have **variety** in a store? Why or why not?

7. What kind of things are kept in a **wallet**. Make a list.

8. If you were a **customer** in a store and saw a bear, what would you do?

**Extra:** Can you think of some more shopping words? Make a list.